Christmas Possibilities

Christmas Possibilities

For Every Day of the Year

BRIAN DEL TURCO

CHRISTMAS POSSIBILITIES

Copyright © 2013 by Brian Del Turco

www.christmaspossibilities.com

ISBN 978-0615939025

Published by TrueNorth Ink.
Printed in the United States of America.
For worldwide distribution.

Contents

Preface

Nothing quite shakes things up like the Christ Child! Is there any time of the year like Christmas? Has any solitary life had such influence?

Jesus uses desire and longing to draw us to His side. Our personal destiny is released, and we are empowered to live our highest life. He's a spell-breaker—the Son who has been given will liberate you, opening the door to the life you were meant to live.

It's said that good things happen on the dance floor. Intimacy is born, a bright future is seen. We've been unaware of the sacred dance, the interplay between heaven and earth. Christmas is about a new relationship with heaven that changes everything, now and forever.

And here's some good news. Christmas possibilities are meant to be experienced every day of the year!

So this comes with prayer, that as you read and reflect, you will experience the peace and goodwill of God toward you in the weeks and months ahead ...

Brian Del Turco

Listen to Your Heart

"It would seem that our Lord finds our desires not too strong, but too weak. We are half-hearted creatures ... far too easily pleased." ~ C.S. Lewis

Angela closed the shop door behind her and stepped into the crisp autumn air. With the Holidays approaching, her hope was to discover something new for the home. Nothing specific in mind. She wasn't even quite sure what she wanted.

When I see it, I'll know, she thought.

But she couldn't find anything, at least not now. There was still time to squeeze in her fitness walk at the park before dinner.

The Virginia foliage was peaking ... bright yellows, burnt oranges, and vivid crimson. With her one year-old daughter sleeping in the stroller, she briskly made her way through the walkways. The thoughts and emotions were welling up again, the natural beauty only seeming to nourish her reflective mood.

What is this low-grade ache, this longing that keeps coming around? Not finding something for the home … well, it's just a perfect picture of my life! Why do things feel so incomplete? This is crazy. Will my desires ever be satisfied? I love Christopher. I adore my daughter. I'm so grateful to be married, to start a family. I just know my friends would think I'm crazy if they really knew my feelings.

It was a familiar pattern of thoughts, awakened from time to time …

Christopher was making his way home. This stretch of roadway usually made Angela's husband feel alive, though the Blue Ridge Mountains weren't doing their magic on this day.

At times, he felt a real sense of personal empowerment. The world as he knew it seemed to be his, and his life-horizons seemed to glow with light. On other days, *diminished* would be a word describing how he felt.

He had taught for several years, recently completing his masters degree. Now, he was an assistant principal for a Middle School. Significant mile-markers were reached in their lives after high school. Angela earned her bachelor's degree in social work. There was their engagement and a beautiful wedding celebrated by family and friends. A healthy, growing marriage. The beginning of a career in education for Christopher. First child. First home. He and Angela were part of a good church, and were enjoying several close friendships with other couples.

All of these things were wonderful, and yet, Christopher, too, was questing.

Maybe I should talk with someone. I can't shake this passion for inner cities. Or, is it developing nations? … I'm not certain. I want us to meet new people, experience new places. I'm craving new seasons. I have a beautiful wife whom I deeply love. I always looked forward to beginning a family. Some of my old friends have little of this. Some have none of it! And yet I can't seem to be satisfied? Sometimes I envy. What am I chasing? Am I self-absorbed?

'Higher Up' and 'Further Back'

I'm sure there are times we can all relate to what Angela and Christopher are experiencing.

C.S. Lewis wrote of a longing, a questing for something from which we are separated.[1] Have you ever felt disconnected from your authentic life—the life you're meant to live? I know I have. And I don't think I'm alone at all. Good things are happening. And I'm grateful. It's just I know there's more.

We sense something is incomplete and unfinished ...

Sehnsucht (ZANE-zoocht) is a German word which captures the searching of the human heart: *yearning, craving, and life's longings.* It can feel like a desire for a distant country, a place we somehow know is familiar, a place we're meant to be.[2] We continue to search for happiness, all while trying to deal with the reality of desires not yet fulfilled.

It's a small thing. Angela just wants to discover something new and bring it into their home. And yet, on this day, it seems she's thwarted. Even if she did find that something, would it really touch the deeper parts of her heart? Often stirred by these types of experiences, our hearts may be seeking to convey a deeper message to us. What is her heart trying to say? Will something new in the home satisfy her?

An event, a conversation, a piece of music, a movie, something we read, a walk, a memory, a face, a season ... these and more can stir desire and longing, causing it to rise in our consciousness. Lewis sees it as the *"inconsolable secret."*

Christopher is not merely trying to make it home after a day at the school. What he is really questing for is a home beyond their "first home"—his true, authentic place in life.

As he grows in his walk with Christ, there is something he cannot seem to avoid. He must know that his personal life story is written within the Greater Story from above. He is after adventure. Adventure touched by something much larger than himself.

For all the anticipation and beauty of Christmas, it is often a season of desire and longing. What's good and beautiful in our lives is highlighted during this time of year. What's not so good is also magnified. Life-desires we carry throughout the year seem to rise within us in bold relief. We can experience feelings of anticipation and joy, as well as disappointment.

Truly, all that is good and beautiful in our experience gives us a vision and thirst for more. All of it taken together is a sign pointing us to something more wonderful still.

The truth is that nothing in this earth can finally satisfy us. Much can make us content for a time but nothing can fill us to the brim. The reason is that our final joy lies "beyond the walls of this world," as J.R. Tolkien put it. Ultimate beauty comes not from a lover or a landscape or a home, but only through them. These earthly things are solid goods, and we naturally relish them. But they are not our final good. They point to what is higher up and further back.... We human beings want God even when we think that what we really want is a green valley, or a good time from our past, or a loved one. Of course we do want these things and persons, but we also want what's behind them.[3]

This is the place where Angela and Christopher are in their journey. They may not yet articulate it clearly, but this is what is moving in their hearts. As we are honest with ourselves, we know we're no different. We cannot help but reach for what is "higher up" and "further back."[4] Our hearts are relentless. We are drawn to Someone. And we are drawn to our highest life, a life which only He can bring us into.

The Blessing of a Restless Heart

Augustine (354-430 AD) once prayed, "Grant me chastity, but not yet." He spent years of his life trying to satisfy human longing and desire, both on the dark side and on the side of light. Eventually, David's cry in Psalm 42 shaped his quest.

> *"As the deer longs for streams of water, so I long for you, O God. I thirst for God, the living God. When can I go and stand before him?"* [5]

What Augustine came to understand about the human heart is that it is searching for God. The famous prayer at the beginning of his *Confessions* is timeless and universal—*"O Lord, you have made us for yourself, and our heart is restless until it rests in you."*

You see, it's a matter of design.

The Rolling Stones, released a single in 1965, their first #1 hit in the United States. The music of a culture is a window into its soul. There's a reason their song resonated with so many. The lyrics of *Satisfaction* spoke of their weariness and frustration with commercialism and sexuality. *"I can't get no satisfaction, I can't get no satisfaction, cause I try and I try and I try and I try."*

Rock and roll. Sex. Drugs. Wealth. They simply could not arrive at a place of peace.

Our heart is designed for the Creator. And apart from Him, the full beauty of our lives cannot flower. Angela and Christopher are followers of Christ. They're certainly not living the lifestyle of Augustine before he came to faith, or Mick Jagger in our time. Yet, even so, there is always a thirst for a deeper intimacy with God, and a hunger for more of the personal story they are designed to experience.

Our restlessness may cause us to look to the past with nostalgia. But seasons have changed. Places are different. People often change. We cherish the good memories, yet a deeper joy is not found by gazing backward. We look to the future with hope and anticipation. Many of the things we desire are good. Yet, we must appreciate that our longings are gracefully pointing us to our Ultimate Joy. He longs to flow through our desires with His Presence, and His Dream.

We need mystery in life. And this is a wonderful mystery.

God is good. Our part in His Dream is the highest life we can live. The satisfaction of our desire and longing is discovered in the long-awaited Gift. The story of our lives is wrapped in the Son who has been given. So we welcome our restless heart as a blessing.

1. Our heart keeps us questing for Him, our Ultimate Joy and Satisfaction. *"You will make known to me the path of life. In Your presence is fullness of joy. In Your right hand there are pleasures forever."*[6] Everything good in life, and throughout eternity, flows from Him.

2. And our restless heart keeps us venturing for His best in our lives. We learn that we discover our true selves through our yieldedness to Him.

Christmastime Is Here

No event in human history is more dramatic and consequential than the incarnation of God's Son—nothing is even remotely close. The Christmas story changes everything. Earth has been reconnected with heaven in a new way, and we can experience things we have not imagined.

Both now and forever.

"... things which eye has not seen and ear has not heard, and which have not entered the heart of man, all that God has prepared for those who love Him. For to us God revealed them through the Spirit; for the Spirit searches all things, even the depths of God."[7]

Christmastime is here. All year.

I believe we will discover powerful and fulfilling ways of living, seen within the accounts of Christ's birth in Matthew and Luke. Christmas is not meant to be enjoyed for one day, or even for a season, for we can live in the light and potential of Christmas every day of the year!

Visit the Christmas Possibilities website at
www.christmaspossibilities.com

Life Reflection

Time spent in personal reflection is time well invested. What may your heart be saying?

- *Are there ways you can relate to what Angela and Christopher are sensing?*

- *Can you open up to the thought that the "low-grade ache" you may experience from time to time—the longing in life you carry—is a faithful message to your life? Are you ready to discover your heart's message?*

- *Will you see your restless heart as a gift? … an elegant invitation to quench your thirst in Christ, to be drawn into His Dream?*

Prayer & Affirmation

How can a single prayer be measured? Is there anything more creative than prayer?

Father, I stand before you in the name—
on the merits of your Son, Jesus Christ.
I bring my longing, restless heart before you.
Soften and shape the stony parts of my heart.
Create within me a receptiveness to your Dream.
I thirst for You ...
Lead me to drink from the river of your Presence,
from the streams of your Dream.
For You are my joy.
And you richly give me all things to enjoy.

I'm grateful now and forever.

Amen.

Notes

1. C.S. Lewis wrote about this in different writings, for example, *The Weight of Glory*.

2. Lewis, *The Weight of Glory*.

3. Cornelius Plantinga, Jr., *Engaging God's World: A Christian Vision of Faith, Learning, and Living* (Grand Rapids, MI: William B. Eerdmans Publishing Company, 2002), 6.

4. Lewis, *The Weight of Glory.* "Higher up" and "further back" ... ultimately, we are reaching for God. We are reaching "back" to Him in the sense of reaching for the Garden of Eden, the intimacy we had with Him, desiring our original design and place. I also think of reaching "higher up" and "further back" as understanding the Creator was thinking of us before we were born, even before the world was created.

5. Psalm 42:2 NLT

6. Psalm 16:11 NASB

7. 1 Corinthians 2:9-10 NASB

Breaking the Spell ...
Discovering the
True You

"How much happier you would be, how much more of you there would be, if the hammer of a higher God could smash your small cosmos." ~ G.K. Chesterton

As long as Prince Rilian in C.S. Lewis' *The Chronicles of Narnia* is under the spell of the witch's sorcery, he cannot recall where he came from or who he was. He felt it as a *"heavy, tangled, cold, clammy web of evil magic."*

I wonder how many people feel this way.

Of course the witch told him this was his "right mind." When he did have clarity, he was told those were moments of insanity. Clearly, the Enemy opposes the discovery, development, and deployment of the true self.

I believe our quest for personal identity and significance is the most powerful drive we have. And I believe it's inextricably connected to the Creator. Os Guinness says, "Calling is the most comprehensive reorientation and the most profound motivation in human experience—the ultimate Why for living in all history."[1]

Do You Feel Powerful?

One of the greatest things we all share is the felt-need to live powerfully. Deep within, we long to live with authentic power.

Human history is filled with questing for power and meaning. Hesiod was an early Greek poet. He dreamed of a lost Golden Age from the past, even as he saw no hope looking forward. The Roman poet Virgil actually sang of one who would deliver the world from its sufferings and by whom "the great line of the ages begins anew."[2] The "line of the ages" beginning anew? This sounds a lot like the "restoration of all things" the Scriptures speak of.[3] These traces of longing and desire seem to be timeless and universal.

One of the leading things that made Jesus Christ so attractive is that he empowered the human condition. He healed people of their sickness, released individuals from demonic bondage, and raised people from the dead to a new life.

And this is significant—He released people from their false selves, opening the door to their true identities. Jesus Christ not only did these things in the past, as seen in the Gospels of the New Testament ... He continues to do them today. For He is the same, yesterday, today, and forever.[4]

"With God's Help I Shall Become Myself"

So what about living from the true self? How are we doing?

When our lives are disoriented, they don't make sense. What's shocking is that even self-identified Christians are not doing well with identity and personal meaning. An outcome from a study by Barna research was that Christians and non-Christians were equally likely to be seeking meaning and purpose in life.[5]

There is a depth and weightiness *(a glory, brilliance, splendor, and beauty)* to your life waiting to be deeply discovered. Your true self brings pleasure to the Creator and deep joy to you. How do we get accurate about it? Clarity is a high value with the Creator. How can we discover clarity about our true passion and purpose, about His dream for our lives?

As Soren Kierkegaard said, "Now with God's help I shall become myself."

Story, Desire, and Journey

Calling is nuanced and multi-layered. This human being thing can be pretty complicated! But we can know that the Creator is speaking and has our best interests at heart.

In *It's Your Call: What Are You Doing Here?*, Gary Barkalow writes about three coordinates that guide us with our calling.[6]

1. *Personal story*
2. *The desires of our heart*
3. *Our journey in life*

Will you see yourself as an explorer, a navigator? We become more self-aware, acquiring our bearings by triangulating these three reference points, as we journey in life.

How could things change if we connected with the *power of story* in our personal lives? In story, there is a sequence, a flow, a plot. Our personal storyline helps us look forward with an expectation of good, providing identity and direction. Here's the mystery—the story of our lives fits within the Larger Story of the Creator. We need that setting and context. In this way, we learn to overcome and become who we really are. We progressively read and live from a beautiful script as we walk with God.

Intense desire is something we may need to become more comfortable with. Many times we fail to appreciate that God leads us through the desires He has placed within us. Eventually, from the deepest part of our authentic selves, we discover we are supposed to do what we most want to do. It's a process, and it can be messy to unearth authentic desire. But it's quite worth it to experience the true self.

And what about our *life-journey?* It's in our interests to journey with the Creator. "Blessed is the man whose strength is in You, whose heart is set on pilgrimage ... they go from strength to strength; each one appears before God in Zion."[7] Our life-journey talks to us and shapes us.

God uses story, desire and journey, and he is speaking through it all. Hopefully we are listening. But we need something more ...

"A Light of Revelation" Has Been Given

All around the birth of Christ is extraordinary guidance from heaven. It's everywhere.

- The wise men from the East were led by the star, and then by divine warning in a dream.
- Gabriel manifested to Zacharias in the Temple, speaking of the birth of John the Baptist, the one who would prepare the way for Christ.
- Gabriel visited Mary and spoke to her of a supernatural conception. The expected Messiah would come through her womb.
- An angel of the Lord appeared to Joseph in a dream, revealing to him that Mary indeed was pregnant by supernatural means.
- The lowly shepherds encountered angel armies in the night skies above the Judean hills, receiving a special birth announcement.

- Simeon and Anna were in touch with the Holy Spirit on a daily basis. They were precisely led to identify the Christ Child when Joseph and Mary brought Him to the Temple as an infant.

Simeon prophesied that Jesus was a "light of revelation."[8] When Zacharias' tongue was loosed, he spoke of the *Dayspring (literally, the Dawn)* who has visited us ... "to give light to those who sit in darkness and the shadow of death, to guide our feet into the way of peace."[9]

Mystery in our lives is an invitation to become intimate with God. Receiving revelation breaks the spell over our lives, empowering us to comprehend and experience our true identity.

The Spirit of Wisdom and Revelation

To be merely a child of the Enlightenment—living from a level of human rationalism and reason, alienated from divine suggestion, promptings, and revelation—is to be stunted in total human development. Yes, I'm well aware that thought is offensive to many in today's culture! But I believe you cannot be a fully developed human being without hearing from the Creator!

There is an ancient, powerful prayer that will transform your life. Pray this prayer for twenty-one days and your perception will begin to change. I believe you will begin to sense things shifting, starting to move in a beautiful direction.

Can you imagine coming into a prayer of agreement with the Apostle Paul? Well, millions of believers since the first century have prayed several great apostolic prayers from the New Testament. One of these prayers is in the letter to the Ephesians.

"I do not cease giving thanks for you, while making mention of you in my prayers; that the God of our Lord Jesus Christ, the Father of glory, may give to you a spirit of wisdom and revelation in the knowledge of Him. I pray that the eyes of your heart may be enlightened, so that you will know what is the hope of His calling ... "[10]

Ask for an increased level of the spirit of wisdom and revelation in the knowledge of Christ—the Holy Spirit, the Spirit of Christ.

Prayers are eternal. They never die. And they are cumulative, building over time. Paul's prayer for the Ephesian believers is still before the throne of grace, rising as an eternal incense. Let's pray this same prayer with the apostle Paul, along with millions of believers over the centuries since the time of the early church. Ensure that your prayer incense is there. Now that's a prayer of agreement!

The *spirit of wisdom and revelation* is experienced in our relational knowledge of Jesus Christ. It's not a cerebral, cognitive knowledge of Christ, as well as the truth He communicates. It's a relational, heart knowledge.

Everything you need and truly want is wrapped in the person of Jesus Christ. Everything you need to know is in the mind of Christ. I'm not entirely sure about bumper sticker theology. But if we must adhere theology to our vehicles, let's consider placing *Jesus is Brilliant* right next to *Jesus is Lord.* Dallas Willard writes in *The Divine Conspiracy* that surely Jesus must be amused at what Nobel Prizes are awarded for today.

[Jesus] is now supervising the entire course of world history (Revelation 1:5) while simultaneously preparing the rest of the universe for our future role in it (John 14:2). He always has the best information on everything and certainly also on the things that matter most in human life.[11]

Jesus—*resurrected, ascended, and enthroned*—has consummate mastery over every aspect of reality. He has every answer and solution we need or want. And in every sphere: personal, family, business, community, and society. What information do you need from Him? Is there something in your life or sphere of influence that requires the brilliance and mastery of Jesus?

Do you desire the good life, and to be truly blessed?

Life Reflection

What is your experience with personal identity and calling? What do you envision?

- *Like Prince Rilian in The Chronicles of Narnia, have you ever felt you were caught in a "heavy, tangled, cold, clammy web of evil magic?" How did you feel?*

- *Os Guinness wrote, "Calling is the truth that God calls us to himself so decisively that everything we are, everything we do, and everything we have is invested with a special devotion and dynamism lived out as a response to his summons and service."[12] What's happening in your heart after first reading that sentence?*

- *In 'The Divine Conspiracy,' Dallas Willard wrote, "'Jesus is Lord' can mean little in practice for anyone who has to hesitate before saying, 'Jesus is smart.'"[13] Is the thought that Jesus is immensely brilliant a new way of thinking for you? What can it mean for you this week, this month, this year?*

Prayer & Affirmation

"O Lord, you are the portion of my inheritance and my cup; You maintain my lot. The lines have fallen to me in pleasant places; Yes, I have a good inheritance."[14]

Father, I know You have my best interests in mind,
all for your glory.
I am proud to belong to You.
Power belongs to You.
Yet, you share Your power with me.
With Your help, I will truly become myself.
May my personal storyline fit beautifully
into Your Greater Story. That is my joy.
Jesus, You are my light of revelation.
Father, fill me more and more
with the Spirit of Jesus,
the Spirit of wisdom and revelation.
For it's in Your Son,
that I discover my authentic life.
I'm yours.

I will live my life in a way
that brings You joy.

Amen.

Notes

1. Os Guinness, *The Call: Finding and Fulfilling the Central Purpose of Your Life* (W Publishing Group, 1998), 7.

2. George Eldon Ladd, *The Gospel of the Kingdom* (Grand Rapids, MI: William B. Eerdmans Publishing Company, 1959), 14.

3. See Acts 3:19-21

4. Hebrews 13:8

5. Barna Research, *Most People Seek Control, Adventure and Peace in Their Lives,* 2000.

6. Gary Barkalow, *It's Your Call: What Are You Doing Here?* (David C. Cook, 2010).

7. Psalm 84:5, 7 NKJV

8. Luke 2:32 NASB

9. Luke 1:78-78 NKJV

10. Ephesians 1:16-18 NASB

11. Dallas Willard, *The Divine Conspiracy* (HarperSanFrancisco, 1998), 95.

12. *The Call,* 4.

13. *The Divine Conspiracy,* 14.

14. David in Psalm 16:5-6 NKJV

What You Say Makes a Difference

"My Dear Elizabeth: Please don't be afraid. Heaven's promise is so wonderful, I would gladly be mute the rest of my life rather than forfeit what is about to happen." ~ Zacharias

Everyone was celebrating. It had been eight days since the birth, and the humble dwelling was brimming with neighbors and relatives. After a lifetime of barrenness, the Lord had shown favor to the priest and his wife. She had conceived!

The old priest had never felt more alive.

He thought of the meaning of his name—*Yahweh has remembered*—as he recalled the angel's words yet again:

"Do not be fearful, Zacharias. Your requests have been received. Your wife Elizabeth will bear you a son. You are to give him the name John. And you will overflow with joy and gladness, and many will celebrate his birth." [1]

Of course, the guests expected the son would receive the father's name. But Elizabeth said, "No. No, indeed, his name is John." Those in the house were confused. Surely she was mistaken. There was no one in the family named John. The writing tablet was handed to Zacharias ...

'His name is John,' he wrote.

In an instant, an other-worldly energy surged from the crown of his head to the core of his being. The priest's tongue was loosed and he spoke and praised God, the pent-up phrases flowing from deep within.

Fear and awe filled the room. The news would spread to those who lived near the couple, even making it's way throughout the surrounding hill country.

Who would this boy become?

It had been nearly a year since Zacharias was chosen by lot to offer incense in the Temple. He surely would have regarded it as the supreme moment in a lifetime of priestly service. It was an honor that could be received only once, and because of the large number of priests, most never experienced it at all.

The old priest's thoughts returned to Jerusalem, and to his experience in the Temple.

As he had stepped from the Outer Court into the Holy Place, his eyes were drawn to the curtain. Cherubim were woven in scarlet, blue, purple and gold on the thick veil, sixty feet in height. Beyond was the Ark of the Covenant, the blue-white light of God's presence radiating above the mercy seat. Zacharias could not see it, for only the High Priest entered the Holy of Holies on the Day of Atonement each year.

The altar of incense was before the veil, fashioned with acacia wood and overlaid with gold. Incense, representing the prayers of the saints, burned perpetually upon this altar. The rest of the priests and the worshipers remained outside the Holy Place, waiting and praying.

Alone, Zacharias sensed something in the air he had never felt before. It seemed as if time was slowing down. Everything in his being was now drawn to the Altar of Incense. Suddenly, a white light flashed, incomprehensively bright, expelling every shadow from the Holy Place.

Gabriel manifested on the right side of the Altar of Incense. *"Do not be fearful."*

Zacharias swayed, straining to remain upright.

"Stand. Do not be afraid."

Memories and emotions were now swirling in a wind around him as the angel spoke ... *I will have a son? After all this? And he will turn many of Israel's sons back to the Lord? My hope died. It was another lifetime. And He will be a forerunner of the promised Messiah, ministering in the spirit and power of the great prophet? How can I know this for certain? I am old. My wife ... my wife, Elizabeth is weary.*

Gabriel stood in perfect serenity. Zacharias heard himself saying, "How will I know this for certain? For I am an old man and my wife is advanced in years."

What We Say Shapes Our Future

What we believe and say is vital for our lives, and for the storyline God is calling us to live.

Gabriel reaffirmed the words of Malachi, the last words of the Old Testament: "It is he who will go as a forerunner before Him in the spirit and power of Elijah ... to make ready a people prepared for the Lord."[2] Zacharias' response could have been, "Let it be to me according to your word," as Mary would say. He had opportunity to echo the words from heaven.

But he didn't.

Consider that both he and his wife were righteous before God, walking blamelessly in all the commandments of the Lord.[3] Yet, something was in Zacharias that caused his faith to struggle with the message from Gabriel. Seemingly, his faith had weakened through the years of desire and longing. Though he was righteous, perhaps he had a temperament that was challenged with being confident and certain.

And yet, God had chosen he and wife.

Time had matured. Prophecies hundreds of years old were about to be fulfilled. The Messiah was coming, and John, the forerunner, would go before Him. Even so, it was vital that Zacharias speak in harmony with heaven about the conception and birth of John.

The messenger spoke again *"... I am Gabriel. I stand in the presence of the Creator. He sent me to bring this good news to you. Because you did not believe my words, you will be unable to speak until the day comes when this promise is realized."* [4]

Zacharias would not have thought it on this day, but his muteness over the next months would be a gift, an act of grace.

Our Tongue Steers the Course of Our Life

James, the brother of Jesus, said our tongue was like the bridle in a horse's mouth. The powerful animal is controlled by the use of the bridle. He also compared our tongue to a rudder on a ship. Though the vessel is large, and driven by strong winds, it is still directed by the rudder, wherever the pilot desires.[5]

Our tongue steers the course of our life.

James also likened our tongue to a cosmos of iniquity *"... a fire, the very world of iniquity ... and [it] sets on fire the course of our life, and is set on fire by hell."* [6] The destiny we are meant to experience can be singed and even incinerated by our own thoughts and words.

This phrase, *the course of our life* in James 3 is the *wheel of genesis*, or the *wheel of birth*.[7] It is the cycle of creation. Because of our fallen state, the whole cycle of our life and sphere of influence, can be consumed by our speech. We just don't realize how powerful our words are. Our tongue holds the power of life and death.[8]

The good news is the opposite is equally true! When we think and speak in harmony with heaven, we receive and activate the good things God has designed. How good is God? Even as the Israelites were being taken into Babylonian captivity for a time because of their rebellion, God had restoration and new horizons on His mind—"*For I know the thoughts that I think toward you, says the Lord, thoughts of peace and not of evil, to give you a future and a hope.*"[9]

Zacharias led a righteous life. He was told his prayers had been received by God. We admire both he and his wife as choice servants of God. Yet, we also learn from the priest's experience about the importance of our speech. God was not punishing him. God decided He needed to stop Zacharias' disbelieving speech until John was born.

The True Nature of Things

"There are only two ways to live your life. One is as if nothing is a miracle. The other is as if everything is." ~ Albert Einstein

Are we limited by a naturalistic outlook?

It's pretty clear that a naturalistic mindset is the prevailing outlook of our time: *matter is all there is and there is no God who speaks and acts in extraordinary ways on our behalf.* If we're not alert, this way of thinking can begin to seep into our hearts. We become "practical atheists." Yes, we believe in God, but our skepticism and unbelief limits His activity in our everyday lives.

It's as if God is not really present. And active.

As we more clearly understand the true nature of things, we will appreciate the importance of even our own thoughts and words. It's through our faith that we understand how everything came into existence.[10] The Holy Spirit was moving over a chaotic earth at creation—the earth was *sterile and barren, empty, an uninhabitable wasteland.*[11] When God spoke, "Let there be light," the creative process began. It all flowed through the expression of His thoughts. And everything continues to be sustained by His powerful word.[12]

When we appreciate the true nature of things,[13] we value the importance of even our own thoughts and words. Truly we live in such a universe.

> *We are apt to find ourselves saying (or silently thinking), "Things just aren't like that!" But what is it, exactly, that we find wrong? What is amiss with a universe in which reality responds to a word? What is wrong with a universe in which reality responds to thoughts and intentions? Surely we live in precisely such a universe, but our faith does not normally rise to it—or at least not to the extent to which it is true."*[14]

True believers are not naturalists. We're not materialists. And we certainly shouldn't be "practical atheists." Let's allow the Living Word to shape our worldview through the Scriptures. Our thoughts and words do matter ... for when we think and speak in union with the Creator, heaven's design is released in the earth.

Just Say the Word

The Roman centurion's servant was tormented with sickness and ready to die. The centurion loved the servant and sent message to Jesus at Capernaum. The Jewish elders pleaded with Jesus to come and heal the servant because of his love for the nation.

When Jesus was not far from the house, the centurion sent friends to tell Jesus he was not worthy for Him to come into his home. *"But just say the word, and my servant will be healed.*

For I also am a man placed under authority, having soldiers under me. And I say to one, 'Go,' and he goes; and to another, 'Come,' and he comes; and to my servant, 'Do this,' and he does it." [15]

Isn't it amazing that Jesus gave his highest praise about faith recorded in the Gospels to this Roman military man? It was not to Peter or any of the other disciples. Nor was it to the religious establishment of the day. It was to this one who understood how authority worked, and the effectiveness of powerful, belief-filled speech.

Believe What You Say

Faith is movement. Faith is perfected by obedient action.

Jesus also said that faith is belief-filled speaking which flows from a prayerful heart. Peter was absolutely stunned the fig tree Jesus cursed withered and died overnight. So Jesus used the occasion to teach about faith in Mark 11.

1. "Have faith in God" *(verse 22)*.

2. "Speak to the mountain and believe that what you say will happen" *(verse 23)*.

3. "When praying, believe you will receive what you ask for, and you will have it" *(verse 24)*.

4. "When you are praying, if you are holding anything against anyone, release it and forgive them" *(verse 25)*.

Our faith is in God. He is the object, the focal point of our belief *(v. 22)*. Because He is faithful, we can put our faith in Him—He is integrity and fidelity personified! Because He is steadfast, His promises are steadfast. Our faith is not in our faith. It's certainly not in ourselves. It's in nothing other than the person of God and His expressed thoughts. We can feel good about that.

It's intriguing to me that Jesus mentions speaking to the mountain *(v. 23)* before he mentions prayer. Some followers of Christ have weak prayer lives. Other's are more vibrant in prayer, yet don't attain to the level of speaking and declaring in faith that Christ is calling us to. As the Roman centurion understood, the real action is completed in the prayer-borne declaration.

But, if we're to declare words that get results, there's something we need to know. Belief-filled speaking is conceived in the womb of prayer *(v. 24)*. No believing prayer? Then, our words will be stillborn. It's in prayer that our inner person is tuned to Christ's mind, and activated with Christ's energy. We become accurate, knowing what to say. And we draw on Christ's power to back it up!

Supporting all of this is relational integrity. Jesus spoke of two great commandments—loving God, and loving others. The Holy Spirit may bring to our mind a relational issue we need to address in prayer *(v. 25)*. If we're carrying an offense, this is our opportunity to forgive, casting the weight of the issue upon the Lord. He wants it. We may need to personally reconcile with another person. Unforgiveness will short-circuit our prayer power, and when this happens, our speaking power is weakened.

Jesus' desire is that we speak to mountains, moving them out of the way. He wants us to calm storms with authoritative words. He wants us to heal the sick and raise the dead with a word from heaven. His design is for us to declare what the Lord is doing in the earth today.

Truly, how you think, and what you say, makes a difference.

Life Reflection

All things have been created through Christ and for Christ. As we abide in Him, we position ourselves to pray fruitfully, and to speak authoritatively.

- *Like Zacharias and Elizabeth, have you been hoping for something for a long time? What are your top two or three desires?*

- *Consider Dallas Willard's statement on page 36. How may it challenge you to think of reality responding to thoughts and words?*

- *How are you doing with your speech, your faith-language?*

Prayer & Affirmation

"There are degrees of power in speaking the Word of God and prayer is necessary to heighten that power."[16]

~ Dallas Willard

Father, I come boldly to Your throne of grace,
receiving your ability.
I thank you for the gift of asking, the gift of prayer.
As I am lead by your Spirit, and the mind of Christ,
I pray, believing I have received,
and my requests are granted by You.
I give you my capacity for thoughts, words and language.
Use my heart and tongue, I pray,
to release Your design on the earth.

Your will be done on earth as it is in heaven …

Amen.

Notes

1. Luke 1:13-14, author's paraphrase
2. Luke 1:17 NASB
3. Luke 1:6
4. Luke 1:19-20, author's paraphrase
5. James 3
6. James 3:6 NASB
7. Greek meaning, the original language of the New Testament
8. "Death and life are in the power of the tongue, and those who love it will eat its fruit" (Proverbs 18:21 NKJV). Also, see Proverbs 12:13 and 13:3.
9. Jeremiah 29:11 NKJV
10. "By faith we understand that the worlds were prepared by the word of God, so that what is seen was not made out of things which are visible" (Hebrews 11:3 NASB). The spoken word of God *framed* the worlds (NKJV).
11. Genesis 1:2
12. "[He] upholds all things by the word of His power" (Hebrews 1:3 NASB).
13. Physics has been inching toward theology since 1920. Since that time, physicists are increasingly saying that thought or consciousness is behind physical matter. Christian belief says this consciousness is the *Logos*, God's Son, Jesus Christ. See John 1:1-5.
14. Dallas Willard, *In Search of Guidance: Developing a Conversational Relationship With God* (Eugene, OR: Wipf & Stock Publishers, 1997), 136.
15. Luke 7:7-8 NKJV. See the entire account with the Roman centurion in Luke 7:1-10.
16. Dallas Willard, *In Search of Guidance*.

You're Not Limited

"I can do all things through Christ who strengthens me." ~ The Apostle Paul

Ethan barely heard the alarm ...

It was 5:50 AM again. The time would not be so bad. It's just he was stringing together twelve to fourteen hour days in his business startup. His eyes were throbbing and his body felt numb.

When will I get past this?

Still laying in bed, he checked the calendar on his phone, remembering he had a mastermind meeting later that morning. That brought a small amount of energy. The monthly virtual connection with six small business owners was his lifeline these days. The accountability was good, and the exchange of ideas was always motivating and beneficial.

He had finally left his accounting position with a medium-sized company four months ago. When he thought about the past six years, he wondered how he ended up in the accounting field at all. He had only grown increasingly miserable. Accounting was a noble profession, but he came to realize he was working against the grain of who he was. Since his junior year in college, he knew he wanted to be an entrepreneur. But he felt he was too deep into his accounting degree to change his major. He had now left the shoreline of the corporate world, and was sailing the waves of a new start-up.

He felt his business plan was solid. Others he trusted thought so. And he knew the market held massive potential for what he was offering. It was obvious that increasing the client base was the key to experiencing long-term success. Of course new business had to be acquired while keeping current clients happy. He also had to tend to the many administrative details of a new business. As with any start-up, cash flow was always an issue.

Though he knew this was his passion, he couldn't help but admit the stress level was rising. Still … his vision was strong, and his hopes were high.

Supernatural Conception

Ethan is in the throes of a challenging season with his business. Any start-up is challenging. The truth is that whenever we make a move to advance to a higher level in any area (relationships, wellness, career, etc.), we will experience resistance. We wonder if we're going to make it.

Thankfully, we're not limited to our natural means.

In the six month of Elizabeth's pregnancy, the angel Gabriel was sent to Mary in northern Israel, to the city of Nazareth. Coming into the room, the angel said, "Rejoice! You are highly favored! The Lord is with you. You are truly blessed among women."

Her parents were away from the home that morning, taking care of some personal affairs. She was only fourteen and the angel could see she was deeply troubled.

"Do not be afraid, Mary, for you have found favor with God. And behold, you will conceive in your womb and bring forth a Son, and shall call His name Jesus. He will be great and will be called the Son of the Highest. And the Lord God will give Him the throne of His father David. And He will reign over the house of Jacob forever, and of His kingdom there will be no end."[1]

Mary was betrothed to Joseph, but they had not known each other intimately, as they were not yet married. Her question to Gabriel was an obvious one.

How could she possibly conceive?

She could not have imagined a supernatural conception. This would not be of man. The presence and energy of God's Spirit would overshadow her, and the Living Word would come into her being from above. Using an egg in Mary's body, the Son of God would be conceived in human form.

"The Holy Spirit will come upon you, and the power of the Most High will overshadow you; and for that reason the holy Child shall be called the Son of God ... for nothing will be impossible with God."[2]

After a few moments, Mary responded, "I am the Lord's servant. Let it be done to me as you have said."

Possibilities and Means

Most of us live as if what's possible in our lives is directly correlated to our own means.

Possibilities ...

We desire to become something more. We want to deepen our relationships. We have a passion to accomplish something, to see something significant happen. We sense opportunities. We dream.

Our Means ...

Every natural part of our lives. Temperament. Personal history. Education. Experience. Finances and other resources. Who we know.

How would Mary conceive? Here's the reality—when God speaks, all things are possible! His own power will back up what He says.

Gabriel said, "For nothing will be impossible with God." What it really means is *"there is not one spoken word (rhema in the Greek) of God that does not have the inherent power within the word itself to be realized."*[3] The Phillips translation is helpful: *"For no promise of God can fail to be fulfilled."*[4]

When God speaks, His person is breathed into the words. The very essence of who He is comes with His expressed thoughts, His words. Everything He can do is within His words. Jesus would later say, "The words that I speak to you are spirit, and they are life."[5]

Why try to live as mere women and men ... without the Holy Spirit, without the Word from on High? The *breakthrough faith* of Christmas creates an extraordinary expectancy—*it's not of this world!* We are designed to experience the Holy Spirit of God. We are not meant to live by the natural alone, but by every word that proceeds from God.[6]

We can live and move beyond ourselves, for "in Him (Christ) we live and move and have our being."[7] Our means are not in ourselves, others, or what's around us. Our means to experience the impossible are in the Holy Spirit and in what God says!

Unfathomable Power

Enrico Fermi was an Italian physicist who left Italy in 1938. His wife, Laura, was Jewish, and they were escaping the new anti-semitic laws in Italy. After emigrating to the United States, he worked on the Manhattan Project during World War II.

Chicago Pile-1, the world's first nuclear reactor, was located on a squash court under the stands of the original Stagg Field at the University of Chicago. On Dec. 2, 1942, the team Fermi led unleashed the power of the atom for the first time .

When the *Enola Gay* dropped an atomic bomb over Hiroshima, Japan at the end of World War II, energy that was 2000 times more powerful than any bomb in history was released from one-third of an ounce of uranium. A chain reaction accelerated through 80 generations of doubling, all within a few millionths of a second. The temperature at the epicenter of the explosion was the temperature at the core of the Sun, several million degrees Celsius.[8]

This kind of energy and power is nearly impossible to wrap our minds around. Beyond this, though, we need to ask a question—if there is this much energy in such a small amount of matter (one-third of an ounce), how much power does God have who spoke all of the matter within the entire universe into existence?[9]

None of us can imagine what God is capable of. Which means none of can imagine what we're capable of if we give God control of our lives. His power sets off a chain reaction. And with his energy at work within us, there is nothing we cannot do. Unfortunately, our lives don't always reflect that reality.[10]

Paul wrote to the Romans that the gospel of the kingdom is the power of God for salvation.[11] God is love. But He is also power— *"Where the word of a king is, there is power; And who may say to him, "What are you doing?"[12]* His presence and promises in our lives will power through anything that seems "impossible" to us.

See Mary's experience as a template for your own life. If you will welcome the overshadowing of the Holy Spirit over all that concerns you, and if you will receive in faith what God speaks to you, there is absolutely nothing that is impossible.

Receive Your Personal "Annunciation"

You and I need our own personal annunciation from God!

The *Annunciation* is the Christian celebration of Gabriel's announcement to Mary. In a similar way, we need our own personal annunciation from God! Frankly, we need multiple annunciations as we walk with Christ. We have the opportunity to be filled with God's transforming thoughts and words. His promises contain His power within them to be realized!

What is God announcing to you? What do you need Him to say? With Mary, our response is, "May it be to me as You speak." Ponder and say these phrases from the *Magnificat,* Mary's exclamation of praise as she greeted Elizabeth.[13]

"Oh, how my soul praises the Lord. How my spirit rejoices in God my Savior!"

"For the Mighty One is holy, and He has done great things for me."

"His mighty arm has done tremendous things!"

"He has brought down princes from their thrones and exalted the humble."

"He has filled the hungry with good things."

Life Reflection

Jesus said, "With men this is impossible, but with God all things are possible." Meditate on these three elements of questing to experience the "impossible" ...

- Mary found favor with God because of her faithfulness and obedience. God was with her! Those who are in Christ have the righteousness and favor of Christ. *As we practically walk out the righteousness of God in our everyday lives, we activate His favor in our experience in a real-life way.*

- Welcome the overshadowing of the Holy Spirit in your life on a consistent basis. Do not grieve Him with personal disobedience, or a lack of peace in relationships. Increase personal worship in your lifestyle and cultivate fellowship with the Holy Spirit.[14] Seek to *keep in step with the Holy Spirit.*

- Receive the Word into your life in a larger, more expansive way. The Living Word, Christ Himself, will come to you through the written Word, the Scriptures. *Receive His promises to you in faith—both in the Word, as well as the personal promises He speaks to you.*

Prayer & Affirmation

"There are degrees of power in speaking the Word of God and prayer is necessary to heighten that power."[14]
~ Dallas Willard

Father, I come boldly to Your
throne of grace to receive your ability.
I thank you for the gift of asking, the gift of prayer.
As I am lead by your Spirit, and the mind of Christ,
I pray believing that I have received,
and my requests are granted by You.
I give you my capacity for words and language.
Use my tongue, I pray, to release Your design on the earth.

Yours is the kingdom, power, and glory ...

Amen.

Notes

1. Luke 1:30-33 NKJV

2. Luke 1:35, 37 NASB

3. Luke 1:37, author's paraphrase. The original language of the text carries the meaning of "*there is not one spoken word (rhema) of God that does not have the inherent power to be fulfilled.*"

4. Phillips translation

5. John 6:63 NKJV

6. Matthew 4:4; Deuteronomy 8:3

7. Acts 17:28 NKJV

8. Mark Batterson, *Primal: A Quest for the Lost Soul of Christianity* (Colorado Spring, CO: Multnomah Books, 2009), 152.

9. See Psalm 33:6-9; also Romans 4:17 ... "*God, who gives life to the dead and calls into being that which does not exist.*"

10. Batterson, 153.

11. Romans 1:16

12. Ecclesiastes 8:4 NKJV

13. See Luke 1:46-55

14. "The grace of the Lord Jesus Christ, and the love of God, and the fellowship of the Holy Spirit, be with you all" (2 Cor 13:14 NASB).

15. Dallas Willard, *In Search of Guidance: Developing a Conversational Relationship With God* (Eugene, OR: Wipf & Stock Publishers, 1997), 140.

On the Creator's Dance Floor

"Now glory waits so He can enter in, now does the dance begin." ~ Elizabeth Rooney

Simeon was an old man. Tired.

Much of what he knew in his life had died away. It was gone. Even so, a promise remained. He had been told he would live until his eyes rested upon the realization of a long-awaited prophecy ...

> *"For unto us a Child is born, unto us a Son is given; And the government will be upon His shoulder. And His name will be called Wonderful, Counselor, Mighty God, Everlasting Father, Prince of Peace. Of the increase of His government and peace there will be no end."[1]*

Luke writes that Simeon was righteous, waiting for the *Consolation of Israel.*[2] He had been shown he would not die until he saw the promised Messiah.

So he was waiting and longing. *Oh, God, when will my eyes see the promise you have given to the prophets ... the word you have given to me?* It was all so daily for Simeon. Weeks, months, and years passed.

Then, one day, like a thousand days before, he came into the temple in Jerusalem. A new father and mother were bringing their child to perform the prescribed custom according to the Law.

Because Simeon pleased God with his obedience and faith, he was given the ability to perceive with prophetic insight. The Scriptures say he came in the Spirit into the temple. Greeting the parents, he took the child into his arms.[3]

The *Messiah* was before him. What he had longed for, he was now holding. The old man sensed an extraordinary level of completeness and fulfillment.

"Now Lord, you are releasing Your bond-servant to depart in peace, according to Your word; For my eyes have seen Your salvation, which you have prepared in the presence of all peoples." [4]

He could now peacefully pass into eternity.

The father and mother were amazed. She had carried the life of the Christ Child within her. Soon, the life of her son would penetrate her life in an unforeseen way, this time as the anointed Messiah. Her innermost being would be revealed, healed and restored. Truly, all who truly follow Christ experience this blessing. As Simeon prophesied, those who yield will *rise* with Christ—*rise* in this life and throughout eternity. Those who do not, will fall.[5]

At that very moment, a woman appeared. Anna, a prophetess, was eighty-four. Married for just seven years, she had then lived as a widow for decades, never leaving the temple, "serving night and day with fastings and prayers."[6]

The wrinkled prophetess looked upon the fresh face of the teenage mother. Perhaps she took the infant from the arms of Simeon as she wept and gave thanks. As the Holy Spirit moved upon her, she spoke to all who were looking for the Messiah and the redemption of Jerusalem.[7]

The Dance Between Heaven and Earth

Over the past several years I've been intrigued by a growing awareness, an understanding about the present relationship between heaven and earth. Do we believe we're just going to heaven some day? Or is there an interplay, a sacred dance, between heaven and earth right now?

Have we undervalued our place, our role, in the Grand Scheme of things? I believe there is much more than we've known and experienced. One of the greatest values of the inspired Scriptures is they preserve the real-life stories of people of faith. These accounts show us how God relates to us. They show us opportunity—what is possible for us too.

Consider an incident with Israel in the Old Testament.

The people were corrupting themselves by worshiping the golden calf while Moses was on the mountain with God.[8] They had come from Egypt where the calf was worshiped. The people were sacrificing to it, and saying, "This is your god, the god who brought you out of Egypt!"

Of course, they had just been miraculously delivered from slavery and torment by the one true God! So, God says to Moses to leave Him alone so that His anger could burn against the people. He would destroy them and start a new nation with Moses. What strikes me is that God says, "Now let me alone." Well, Moses did not leave God alone. He intercedes in prayer for the people and appeals to God's reputation and Story.

And God changed his mind! It's astonishing. God intends to do something, and he does not want Moses to dissuade Him.

If we will perceive with our faith-understanding, we will see similar experiences from Genesis through the New Testament. And we can experience the same relationship between heaven and earth in our day as well.

Mary Was Not the Only One Expecting

I believe Simeon and Anna were on the dance floor with God. They knew God intimately and were able to move to the rhythm and cadence of the Holy Spirit.

In a powerful sense, Simeon and Anna were just as pregnant with the Christ-Child as Mary was. Empowered and led by the Holy Spirit, they were in a high state of expectancy. They were choice people of prayer. Finely tuned.

The Holy Spirit rested upon Simeon in a remarkable way. Undoubtedly, he invested belief and prayer into what he expected. He was sustained by the promise. He could not die until the word he had been given was realized. Because he was a person of revelation, he was able to bring clear definition and affirmation when Joseph and Mary came to the temple with the Christ Child.

Anna had a clear prophetic edge as well. She led a consecrated lifestyle of worship, fasting and prayer. Overflowing with gratitude, she was able to declare the purpose of God. She spoke to those who were expecting the Messiah—there were others in addition to Simeon and Anna who were steadfast in their expectation.

Now here's a question for us: does God do anything in the earth without revealing it to someone—without obedience, worship, prayer, and prophecy opening the way?

"Surely the Lord God does nothing unless He reveals His secret counsel to His servants the prophets."[9] God asked Himself if He should hide from Abraham what He was about to do.[10] John Wesley boldly said, "God does nothing except in response to believing prayer."

Could it be God's design, his *modus operandi* if you will, that he will not do anything in the earth apart from a consecrated faith-response in someone, or in some group of people? From the Garden of Eden onward, it surely seems the Creator works in partnership with humanity in this way.

"When the fullness of time came, God sent forth His Son, born of a woman."[11] God had His people of faith on the earth who were sensitive to the times, in a high state of expectancy as they watched and prayed. Even the incarnation was surrounded with a faith-response on the earth!

You're Meant to Be on the Dance Floor

We, too, are called to lead our lives in a heightened state of expectancy. We anticipate the coming of Christ again at the Second Advent. But, we also expect those things he is leading us to believe for and experience now. Our present experience is part of His unfolding Story.

The reality is we are meant to taste and experience the powers of the Age to Come in our present time![12] Something of the future is here now … for those who believe.

Christ comes to us with an increasing measure of his abiding presence and influence in our world. The dynamic of the incarnation continues in those in whom Christ abides.

What are you expecting?

The Apostle Paul wrote to the church at Galatia, "I am again in labor until Christ is formed in you."[13] What are you believing for? Are you steadfast in your belief for the promises God gives through His Son? What are you meant to carry and bring into this world?

"Sing, O childless woman, you who have never given birth! Break into loud and joyful song, O Jerusalem, you who have never been in labor. For the desolate woman now has more children then the woman who lives with her husband," says the Lord. "Enlarge your house; build an addition. Spread out your home, and spare no expense!"[14]

I like that … "Spread out your home and spare no expense!"

Be encouraged. You will be stretched. You will be enlarged! There is a creative, faith-shaped tension between the promise he gives you and its fulfillment. It's in this space between the promise and its realization that he forms us, enlarging our capacity to receive, carry, and release his intent in our personal world, as well as the world-at-large.

It's said that good things happen on the dance floor. Intimacy born. A new future begun.

Dance with heaven.

Now is the shining fabric of our day torn open,
flung apart, rent wide by love.
Never again the tight, enclosing sky,
the blue bowl or the star-illumined tent.
We are laid open to infinity, for Easter love
has burst His tomb and ours.
Now nothing shelters us from God's desire—
not flesh, not sky, nor stars, not even sin.
Now glory waits so He can enter in.
Now does the dance begin.

~ Elizabeth Rooney, The Opening

Life Reflection

It is impossible to please God without faith (Hebrews 11:6). Heaven's best comes in response to those who awaken God's pleasure. It is worth our best response of obedience and faith.

- *Is the "dance" between heaven and earth a new way of thinking for you? Are you open to it?*

- *John Wesley's statement, "God does nothing except in response to believing prayer," has big implications for one's worldview? Do you agree or disagree?*

- *Read Isaiah 54:1-2 again. Do you think God may be stretching you? In what ways?*

Prayer & Affirmation

The Adversary is completely powerless when facing steadfast obedience and faith. The flow from heaven to earth is unhindered.

Heavenly Father,
in the name of your son, Jesus Christ,
I ask you to bring my faith to a place of maturity.
Jesus, you are the author and perfecter of my faith.
Stretch me. Enlarge my capacity.
Holy Spirit, lead me in the Sacred Dance.
I pursue a higher state of expectancy,
believing for all that You have promised.

And I stand in this place of expectancy,
drawing to the earth what heaven intends.

Amen.

Notes

1. Isaiah 9:6-7 NKJV
2. Luke 2:25
3. Luke 2:27-28
4. Luke 2:29-31 NASB
5. Luke 2:33-35
6. Luke 2:37
7. Luke 2:38
8. See the account in Exodus 32
9. Amos 3:7 NASB
10. Genesis 18:17
11. Galatians 4:4 NASB
12. Hebrews 6:5
13. Galatians 4:19 NASB
14. Isaiah 54:1-2 NLT

The Advance of Advent

"Why do the nations rage, and the people plot a vain thing?...
Yet I have set My King on My holy hill of Zion." ~ Psalm 2

Herod, an Idumean, was appointed by Rome as the "King of the Jews" in Judea. As long as the Romans were satisfied, he remained in power. He has been called "the evil genius of the Judean nation."[1] A ruthless schemer, he had murdered friends and relatives, as well as enemies. By his orders, one of his ten wives and two of his sons were killed.

The nights were the worst for Herod. Flavius Josephus, a Jewish historian, wrote that Herod was ravaged by pain in his later life.[2] Recently, though, it was not just the physical pain that was keeping him awake. The visiting magi had not returned to report to Herod as agreed upon. He was in the grip of his well-known paranoia and suspicion.

The magi were wise men from Persia in the East, experts in astrology, astronomy, and natural science. Their knowledge of the Hebrew scriptures was most likely traced back to the time of Daniel, who was appointed chief administrator over the wise men of Babylon during the Babylonian captivity.[3] Tradition says there were three wise men because of the three gifts presented to Jesus. But there were likely more. It was no small event when they arrived in Jerusalem after traveling for months. "Where is He who has been born King of the Jews? For we have seen His star in the East and have come to worship Him," they asked.[4]

Hearing of their arrival, Herod had gathered together the chief priests and scribes of the Jews, inquiring where the expected Messiah was to be born. This was followed by a secret meeting with the magi. After finding out when the star first appeared to them, Herod sent them to Bethlehem. His scheme was to have the magi return to him when they had located the home of the Child ... "Bring word to me, that I may come and worship Him also."[5]

But he had no intention of worshiping a new king.

The Child-King

As the magi left Jerusalem, they were filled with exceeding joy, following the "star" to the small town of Bethlehem. Balaam, in the time of Israel's wandering in the wilderness, prophesied of a star: "I see Him, but not now; I behold Him, but not near; A Star shall come out of Jacob; A scepter shall rise out of Israel ...."[6] Surely Daniel, and probably the magi, would have known of this Old Testament prophecy.

Some have speculated there was an alignment of planets in the sky. We know there was a conjunction of the planets Jupiter and Saturn sometime between 7 and 6 B.C. This may have appeared as an unusual star, a phenomenal event in the heavens.[7] Another view says it could have been an exploding star or supernova. There are accounts of this possibility in 5 B.C.[8]

Perhaps the wise men were led by such phenomena. It seems there must have been something more than mere natural phenomena which led them, though. They were filled with joy by the "star." And they were led specifically to the house in Bethlehem where the young Child was. In addition to any natural phenomena, there must have been a presence —an angelic presence, or more likely, a manifestation of the *Shekinah*, similar to the presence of God which guided the Israelites in the wilderness. Truly, the wise men were supernaturally led to the home of Joseph and Mary.

Mary would have been concerned about their coming. She recalled the words of Simeon in the Temple that a sword would pierce her heart. Word had come to their town of the magi's visit in Jerusalem; Bethlehem was located just several miles to the south of city. And she and Joseph were well aware of what could happen to any perceived threat to Herod's power.

As the magi entered the small house, the Child came to the side of Mary.[9] Jesus was playing with simple, carved wooden toys Joseph had made for him. Seeing Him, they fell before Him in worship. Treasures were opened. Perhaps King Solomon's words were rising in the magi's thoughts ... *"The kings of Tarshish and of the isles will bring presents. The kings of Sheba and Seba will offer gifts. Yes, all kings shall fall down before Him. All nations shall serve Him."*[10]

Gold was brought before Him, a gift for royalty, a symbol of the divine. Frankincense was offered, an aromatic used in sacrificial offerings. And myrrh was presented, in preparation for his death and burial. As always, Mary treasured these experiences within, pondering their meaning.

Massacre of the Innocents

Something in the heavens shifted that night. The magi were divinely warned not to return to Herod. They secretly left Bethlehem, returning to their homeland by another way. An angel appeared to Joseph in a dream, warning him to take the Child and his mother and flee to Egypt for a time. He quickly arose with Mary and Jesus and left Bethlehem.

Herod had now been told the magi had left. The torment in his darkened mind eclipsed the pain in his body. The atmosphere seemed thick with the powers of darkness. Enraged, he called for an assistant. No one could threaten his throne—the Child must be eliminated! Men were dispatched to murder every male child in Bethlehem and the surrounding area, from two years old and under, according to the time the star first appeared to the magi.

Jeremiah's words would be fulfilled again ... first realized in Israel's mourning in Babylonian captivity, and now fulfilled in Herod's crazed attempt to murder the Child King. The anguished voices of mothers and fathers could be heard on the outskirts of Jerusalem.

> *"A voice was heard in Ramah, lamentation, weeping, and great mourning, Rachel weeping for her children, refusing to be comforted, because they are no more."*[11]

The Dragon Is Crushed

God is a winner in every situation—nothing frustrates His counsel.

Immediately after the Fall of humanity, a redemptive promise was set in motion: a Seed would come into the earth through the woman, crushing the head of the deceiver. The serpent heard the Creator say, *"I will put enmity between you and the woman, and between your seed and her seed. He will bruise you on the head ...."*[12] The promised Seed, the Messiah, would come into the earth through a woman.

In the last book of the New Testament, John, a disciple of Jesus, wrote he was in the Spirit on the Lord's Day. Late in life, he had been banished by the Romans to the island of Patmos, a barren, rocky island in the Aegean Sea off the coast of Asia Minor. The island was used as a Roman penal colony, and John was sent there as an old man because of his proclamation of scripture and his testimony of Jesus.

In the later part of the first century, the ascended Jesus came to the island to give him a revelation, showing him something of the past, present, and future. The coming of Jesus Christ into the earth was an existential threat to Satan and his kingdom. John saw the attempt to kill the Seed, the Messiah.

"A great sign appeared in heaven; a woman clothed with the sun, and the moon under her feet, and on her head a crown of twelve stars; and she was with child; and she cried out, being in labor and in pain to give birth" (Revelation 12:1-2 NASB).

This woman pictured in Revelation 12 is a composite view of God's people through time. She is the nation of Israel, through whom the Messianic line came. In the New Covenant, she is the church, releasing Christ's continuous presence and ministry into the world. And, she is Mary, through whom Christ came into the world.

"And the dragon stood before the woman who was about to give birth, so that when she gave birth he might devour her child" (Revelation 12:4 NASB).

Throughout the Old Testament, the dragon, Satan, was always seeking to corrupt or eliminate the Messianic line— at any cost, Christ could not come into the earth. After Mary gave birth to Jesus, Herod, saturated in demonic power, sought to kill the Christ Child. Even today, Satan does what he can to obstruct and diminish Christ's work in the earth. Yet to come, there will be an anti-Christ, vainly seeking to "abort" God's plan.

We Overcome!

If you are a child of God through Christ, you cannot be defeated! As we are obedient to the Word, and keep in step with the Spirit, we are always led in the triumph of Christ.[13] The DNA of Christ and His kingdom simply cannot lose.

> *"And she gave birth to a son, a male child, who is to rule all the nations with a rod of iron; and her child was caught up to God and to His throne ... And there was war in heaven, Michael and his angels waging war with the dragon. The dragon and his angels waged war, and they were not strong enough, and there was no longer a place found for them in heaven. And the great dragon was thrown down, the serpent of old who is called the devil and Satan, who deceives the whole world; he was thrown down to the earth, and his angels were thrown down with him"* (Revelation 12:5, 7-9 NASB).

The dragon and his angels are not strong enough—there is no longer a place for them in heaven. They have no authentic standing. They have the capacity to deceive and to tempt. But due to the fall of humanity, whatever authority Satan was given has been stripped from him![14]

> *"Now the salvation, and the power, and the kingdom of our God and the authority of His Christ have come, for the accuser of our brethren has been thrown down, he who accuses them before our God day and night. And they overcame him because of the blood of the Lamb and because of the word of their testimony, and they did not love their life even when faced with death"* (Revelation 12:10-11 NASB).

In Christ, we overcome! We win by the blood of the Lamb. We win by the word of our testimony. And we win by not loving our own lives, even if it means facing death.

The serpent of old, Satan, cannot stop the potential of Christmas in your life ... every day of the year! For the potential of Christmas is the potential of Christ.

Herod's Ugly Demise

Herod died in Jericho after a thirty-seven year reign. His illness at the end—sometimes called "Herod's Evil"—was excruciatingly painful and obvious to all.

Josephus wrote that Herod, ever preoccupied with himself and his ambitions, gave orders that a group of distinguished men should come to Jericho and forcibly placed in the hippodrome. Soldiers were to shoot them with darts at the time of his death to ensure there would be grieving throughout Judea when he died. He knew the Jews would not mourn his own death. Fortunately, his sister Salome, and her husband Alexas, who were charged with overseeing the edict, did not follow through after Herod died.[15]

Herod was under the influence of Satan. He is a picture of Satan's blinding pride, selfish ambition, and evil schemings … he is also a clear picture of Satan's ugly decline and demise. Isaiah spoke of a time soon to come concerning Satan.

> *"Those who see you will gaze at you, and consider you, saying: 'Is this the man who made the earth tremble, who shook kingdoms, who made the world as a wilderness and destroyed its cities, who did not open the house of his prisoners.'"*[16]

Jesus says, "I saw Satan fall like lightning from heaven. Behold, I give you the authority to trample on serpents and scorpions, and over all the power of the enemy, and nothing shall by any means hurt you."[17]

The Child-King: No Longer In a Manger!

When John received the revelation of Jesus Christ on the island of Patmos, he saw and experienced the Son of Man as the ascended Christ.

> *"Then I turned to see the voice that was speaking with me. And having turned I saw seven golden lampstands; and in the middle of the lampstands I saw one like a son of man, clothed in a robe reaching to the feet, and girded across His chest with*

a golden sash. He head and His hair were white like white wool, like snow; and His eyes were like a flame of fire. His feet were like burnished bronze, when it has been made to glow in a furnace, and His voice was like the sound of many waters. In His right hand He held seven stars, and out of His mouth came a sharp two-edged sword; and His face was like the sun shining in its strength" (Revelation 1:12-16 NASB).

This is not the baby Jesus in the manger! Our understanding of Christ must go beyond the earthly perspective. The New Testament is an unfolding, progressive revelation of Jesus Christ. He is now the cosmic Christ, preeminent over all things!

Affirm these statements about the preeminence of Christ over all (from Ephesians and Colossians[18])...

"All things have been created through Him and for Him."

"He is before all things and in Him all things hold together."

"He is the beginning, the firstborn from the dead."

"He is raised from the dead and seated at the right hand of the Father in the heavenly places."

"He is far above all rule and authority and power and dominion, and every name that is named, in this age and in the age to come."

"All things have been placed under His feet."

"He is head of the body, the church."

"He has been given as head over all things to the church."

"He will come to have first place in everything."

Our playing small does not serve us well—it's not our highest life. Even more, it does not serve those around us, and the world-at-large. As we widen our perspective, appreciating the advance of Advent, we rise to a new level of living and influence.

Life Reflection

The incarnation of Jesus Christ was heaven's invasion into a lost world—it's the advance of Advent!

- *Have you ever considered that God always wins? What can that mean for you?*

- *How can you apply Revelation 12:11 to your life? "And they overcame him (Satan, the accuser) because of the blood of the Lamb and because of the word of their testimony, and they did not love their life even when faced with death."*

- *Advent is advancing in history. Is it advancing in your life and personal world?*

Prayer & Affirmation

The first Advent was a bad day for the Adversary. And it's only getting worse.

Father, I thank you for sending Your Son.
The head of the dragon has been crushed.
Satan is under our feet!
I praise You that Advent is advancing.
It is advancing in history ...
and it is advancing in my life.
Be strong in me, Jesus.
Be strong through me.
It's Advent every day of the year.
for me, and for all that concerns me!

All glory to Jesus who is victorious
over all!

Amen.

Notes

1. Tierney, John. "Herod: Herod the Great", Catholic Encyclopedia (1910): Herod, surnamed the Great, called by Grätz "the evil genius of the Judean nation" (Hist., v. II, p. 77).

2. Josephus, Jewish historian. After consulting the writings of Herod's court historian, Josephus wrote: "He had a fever, though not a raging fever, an intolerable itching of the whole skin, continuous pains in the intestines, tumors of the feet as in dropsy, inflamation of the abdomen, and gangrene ..."

3. The queen to King Belshazzar: "There is a man in your kingdom in whom is the Spirit of the Holy God. And in the days of your father, light and understanding and wisdom, like the wisdom of the gods, were found in him; and King Nebuchadnezzar your father—your father the king—made him chief of the magicians, astrologers, Chaldeans, and soothsayers" (Daniel 5:11 NKJV).

4. Matthew 2:2 NKJV

5. Matthew 2:8 NKJV

6. Numbers 24:11 NKJV

7. Donald A. Hagner, *Matthew 1–13, Word Biblical Commentary Volume 33a* (Nashville: Thomas Nelson, 1993), 27.

8. Frank J. Tipler, *The Physics of Christianity* (New York: Doubleday, 2007), 140f.

9. Jesus would have been a toddler, nearly 2 years old at this time. The wise men entered the "house" of Joseph and Mary (Mt. 2:11). Herod had determined from the magi the time the star appeared to them (Mt. 2:7). When he had the male children in Bethlehem and the surrounding area put to death, the command was for boys two years-old and under to be killed, according to the time determined from the wise men (Mt. 2:16).

10. Psalm 72:10-11 NKJV

11. Matthew 2:18, NKJV; also Jeremiah 31:15

12. Genesis 3:15. The *protoevangelium* is the first mention of the Gospel in the Scriptures. Satan would bruise Christ's heel, afflicting Him. But, Christ would crush the head of Satan, dealing him a fatal blow. Paul's words in Romans 16:20 are insightful for us: "The God of peace will crush Satan under your feet shortly" (NKJV).

13. 2 Corinthians 2:14 NASB

14. "Having disarmed principalities and powers, He made a public spectacle of them, triumphing over them in it [the cross]" (Colossians 2:15 NKJV).

15. Josephus, *Antiquities*, 17.6.5

16. Isaiah 14:16-17 NKJV

17. Luke 10:18-19 NKJV

18. A powerful exercise is to meditate and prayer over Colossians 1:16-17 and Ephesians 1:17-23. As appropriate, take phrases and sentences from the scriptures and declare them in the first person.

Afterword...
The Christ Child—
'Disruptive Innovation'

From *CHAOS* to *CREATIVITY* ...

See the Spirit of Christ in the first several verses of the Scriptures, hovering over the waters of chaos, drawing out design and beauty. Nothingness and barrenness? It's His playground. As you reflect on Christ, see the Kingly Entrepreneur, creating and multiplying fathomless value from nothingness.

Disruptive Innovation Flowing from Bethlehem Into Your Life

Look to the little town of Bethlehem. Is there anything about the birth of the Christ Child that is not *disruptive, inconvenient,* and yet *innovative*?

* The most misunderstood pregnancy in history ... *disruptive innovation.*

* An imperial decree from Rome that sent everyone to the city of their birth for a census—a 90 mile donkey journey, just as Mary was nearing delivery ... *disruptive innovation.*

* No place for the birth. Laid in an animal feeding trough ...

- The initial birth announcement given to the lowest strata of society, the overnight shepherds ...

- The religious establishment did not know what was happening. Jerusalem was disturbed. A crazed Herod was trying to kill the Christ Child ... *it is all disruptive innovation.*

Disruptive innovation upsets and supersedes our current place in life. It elevates everything to a new level of reality and experience. Flowing from Bethlehem into our time, there's absolutely nothing like the Christ Child to disrupt the status quo.

What About You this Christmastime ... and Throughout the Year?

Surrounded with a good dose of chaos? Rejoice with the angel-armies above the Judean hills—you're perfectly positioned! Celebrate the disruptive innovation of our Creator God! It's a pattern, a beautiful, mysterious pathway into an increasingly creative future.

How should we live in the true spirit of Christmas all year long?

- The knowledge of the Holy One sustains us: know that He purposes to work from chaos to design and beauty.

- Rejoice with expectant faith!

- Welcome the Holy Spirit to overshadow your person, your situation.

- Listen for the creative, heavenly Word to come to you.

- Courageously flow and move forward in the Father's disruptive innovation.

As over the original waters of chaos, and as within the womb of Mary, call for the creative Spirit of God to bring fresh life and innovation! Then ready yourself for transformation.

What Can This Mean for You?

Comprehending the incarnation—the Son of God becoming flesh, descending into time and space as we know it—will radically alter our lives.

Far beyond remembering a baby in a manger, we must appreciate Christmas as a merging of heaven and earth. This changes everything. The incarnation means that heaven and earth have been connected again. Humanity and the cosmos may now be reconciled to the Creator in Christ.

A seamlessness between heaven and earth has been reestablished. This is the grounds on which we can now pray, *"Your kingdom come, Your will be done, on earth as it is in heaven."* God wants to be reconnected with us. He desires for us to partner with Him. The dynamic of the incarnation is now available in our lives!

- Your personal development
- Your family
- Your marriage
- Your calling and work
- Your ministry
- Your legacy

What steps can you take to tap this potential, beginning today?

- We must be born again in Christ. The potential of heaven and earth merging in our lives begins with the born-again experience. Jesus said, "I assure you, unless you are born again, you can never see the Kingdom of God" (Jesus Christ in John 3:3, NLT).

- Allow Christ's abiding presence to expand within you *(increase hospitality to Christ within)*. The born-again experience introduces you to the Kingdom. We now want Christ to dwell *(an incarnation)* within our hearts in an expansive way—"That He would grant you, according to the riches of His glory, to be strengthened with power through His Spirit in the inner man, so that Christ may dwell in your hearts through faith" (Ephesians 3:16-17, NASB).

- The same voice that spoke over the chaotic waters in Genesis, the same Word that was released into Mary's womb ... allow that Word to richly dwell within you. Abide in that Word as a life-force and decree it over all things! Let the word of Christ richly dwell within you, with all wisdom.

Release the potential of the incarnation in you!
And through you!

"God willed to make known what are the riches
of the glory of this mystery among the Gentiles:
which is CHRIST IN YOU, the hope of glory."

~ Colossians 1:27, NKJV

www.christmaspossibilities.com

Visit the *Christmas Possibilities* website for fresh content and announcements ... even in July! For the Christmas possibilities that Jesus brings are for every day of the year.

"For with God nothing will be impossible."

ABOUT THE AUTHOR

Brian Del Turco is a graduate of Oral Roberts University with a Bachelor of Arts in Theological and Historical Studies. He has also studied at the graduate level, focusing on adult education and theology. His experience includes radio announcing, adult Christian education, church planting, and pastoral ministry. Brian and Penelope have been married for over 25 years. He finds entertainment in the facial expressions of those who learn he and his wife have four daughters. Personal interests include American history, culture, writing, teaching, and first-rate coffee.

Made in the USA
Lexington, KY
30 December 2013